D1153434

everyday
smoothies
& juices

Bath · New York · Singapore · Hong Kong · Cologne · Delhi · Melbourne

This edition published by Parragon in 2009

Parragon
Queen Street House
4 Queen Street
Bath BA1 1HE, UK

ISBN 978-1-4075-7844-6

Printed in Indonesia

Cover by Talking Design
Designed by Terry Jeavons & Company
Additional text by Linda Doeser

This book uses both metric and imperial measurements. Follow the same units of measurement throughout; do not mix metric and imperial. All spoon measurements are level: teaspoons are assumed to be 5ml, and tablespoons are assumed to be 15ml. Unless otherwise stated, milk is assumed to be full fat, eggs and individual vegetables are medium, and pepper is freshly ground black pepper.

The times given are an approximate guide only. Optional ingredients, variations or serving suggestions have not been included in the calculations.

Recipes using raw or very lightly cooked eggs should be avoided by infants, the elderly, pregnant women, convalescents, and anyone suffering from an illness. Pregnant and breastfeeding women are advised to avoid eating peanuts and peanut products. Sufferers from nut allergies should be aware that some of the ready-made ingredients used in the recipes in this book may contain nuts. Always check the packaging before use.

everyday
smoothies
& juices

introduction	4
energize	6
revive	48
refresh	90
soothe	124
bliss	166
index	208

introduction

The ancestry of smoothies can be traced back to the milkshake that was so fashionable half a century ago, but their style and phenomenal popularity are thoroughly modern. In all aspects they reflect contemporary preoccupations – they're bursting with flavour, wonderfully refreshing, nourishing and sustaining, free from preservatives and artificial colouring, incredibly quick to make, look fabulous and kids think they're cool.

They may be made with fruit, vegetables or a mixture of both and some include milk, yogurt or similar products. They rarely require extra sweetening and when they do, this is often in the form of honey rather

than refined sugar. Unlike milkshakes, which are usually made with flavoured syrup, smoothies always contain a high proportion of whole fruits or vegetables. The bare minimum of preparation – peeling and removing pips, for example – means not only that smoothies are

very quick to make but that nutrients are not lost and healthy dietary fibre is included in every glass.

As they taste so delicious and are often colourful and attractive, it's easy to encourage the family to consume more fruit and vegetables as nutritionists are constantly recommending. This is good news for parents who may struggle with providing a healthy diet for recalcitrant children and intractable teenagers. They make great anytime-of-day drinks and a fabulous substitute for unhealthy snacks like crisps and biscuits. Depending on the particular ingredients, smoothies can provide an energy boost first thing in the morning and when you need to keep going later in the day, or a calming and refreshing way of winding down and relaxing. Far more exciting than plain fruit juice, they offer a

much better way to quench your thirst than commercial sodas and soft drinks and can form a useful part of a weight-loss plan.

Whether your taste is for sweet or savoury, tangy or creamy, piquant or soothing, there's a smoothie to suit you – and your good health.

energize

While nutritionists advise that breakfast is the most important meal of the day, it still remains the most neglected. In the morning rush, even a slice of toast can seem too much to prepare and teenagers, in particular, are often very negative about eating first thing in the day. Smoothies are the perfect answer – irresistible, quick to make and packed with goodness. Some recipes are particularly good for kick-starting the day – citrus fruits activate the system, while bananas are powerhouses of energy that will keep you going through the whole morning.

When you feel that you're beginning to flag – in the mid afternoon, for example – why not try a reviving smoothie instead of another cup of coffee? Replace the short-lived buzz of caffeine with a high-vitality mix of berries or an antioxidant booster of orange and red vegetables. Better still, take pre-emptive action and include any one of these revitalizing drinks with your lunch to prevent an energy slump later in the day.

Smoothies also make terrific after-school treats. They won't spoil the appetite for family supper, they are much healthier than crisps or sweets and they will help fortify young people to do battle with their homework.

breakfast smoothie

ingredients

SERVES 2

250 ml/9 fl oz orange juice

125 ml/4 fl oz natural yogurt

2 eggs

2 bananas, sliced and frozen

2 small bananas, to decorate

method

1 Pour the orange juice and yogurt into a food processor or blender and process gently until combined.

2 Add the eggs and frozen bananas and process until smooth.

3 Pour the mixture into glasses and decorate with the bananas.

rise & shine juice

ingredients

SERVES 1

4 tomatoes, quartered

85 g/3 oz grated carrot

1 tbsp lime juice

method

1 Put the tomatoes, carrot and lime juice into a food processor or blender and process for a few seconds until smooth.

2 Place a nylon sieve over a bowl and pour in the tomato mixture. Using a spoon, gently push as much of the liquid through the sieve as possible. Discard any pips and pulp remaining in the sieve.

3 Pour the juice into a glass and serve immediately.

banana breakfast shake

ingredients

SERVES 2

2 ripe bananas

200 ml/7 fl oz low-fat natural yogurt

125 ml/4 fl oz skimmed milk

$1/2$ tsp vanilla essence

method

1 Put the bananas, yogurt, milk and vanilla essence into a food processor or blender and process until smooth.

2 Serve at once.

breakfast berry smoothie

ingredients

SERVES 1–2

200 g/7 oz strawberries
100 g/3$\frac{1}{2}$ oz raspberries
100 ml/3$\frac{1}{2}$ fl oz soya milk
40 g/1$\frac{1}{2}$ oz unsweetened muesli

method

1 Reserve a strawberry for decoration, then process or blend the remainder with the raspberries.

2 Add the juice to the food processor with the soya milk and muesli, and process until almost smooth.

3 Pour into glasses, top each smoothie with half a strawberry and serve.

tropical sunrise

ingredients

SERVES 1–2

1 ripe mango
1 orange
$1/2$ pomegranate

method

1 Remove the stone and peel from the mango, and peel the orange. Process or blend them together and pour into glasses.

2 Peel the pomegranate, reserve 1 tablespoon of the seeds and blend the rest.

3 Pour the pomegranate pulp into the orange and mango juice and sprinkle with the reserved pomegranate seeds.

wake-up juice

ingredients

SERVES 1–2

1 orange
large sprig of fresh mint
200 g/7 oz cantaloupe melon flesh
sprigs of mint, to decorate

method

1 Peel the orange, leaving on the white pith.

2 Process or blend the orange, mint and melon.

3 Pour into glasses and serve decorated with sprigs of mint.

berry brightener

ingredients

SERVES 2

175 g/6 oz blueberries
150 ml/5 fl oz cranberry juice
150 ml/5 fl oz natural yogurt
honey, to taste (optional)

method

1 Put the blueberries and cranberry juice into a processor or blender and process for 1–2 minutes, until smooth.

2 Add the natural yogurt and process briefly to combine. Taste and add honey, if using. Process briefly again until thoroughly blended.

3 Pour into chilled glasses and serve.

blueberry thrill

ingredients

SERVES 2

100 ml/3¹/₂ fl oz Greek yogurt

100 ml/3¹/₂ fl oz water

125 g/4¹/₂ oz frozen blueberries

whole frozen blueberries, to decorate

method

1 Put the yogurt, water and blueberries into a food processor or blender and process until smooth.

2 Pour into glasses and top with whole frozen blueberries.

tropical watermelon smoothie

ingredients

SERVES 2

1 watermelon wedge, about 600 g/1 lb 5 oz

2 small bananas, preferably Lady Fingor

225 ml/8 fl oz coconut cream

method

1 Remove and discard the seeds from the watermelon, then cut the flesh off the rind and chop coarsely. Peel and slice the bananas.

2 Put the watermelon, bananas and coconut cream into a food processor or blender and process until combined.

3 Pour into chilled glasses and serve.

orange & strawberry cream

ingredients

SERVES 2

125 ml/4 fl oz natural yogurt

175 ml/6 fl oz strawberry yogurt

175 ml/6 fl oz orange juice

175 g/6 oz frozen strawberries

1 banana, sliced and frozen

slices of orange and whole fresh strawberries on cocktail sticks, to decorate

method

1 Pour the natural and strawberry yogurts into a food processor or blender and process gently. Add the orange juice and process until combined.

2 Add the strawberries and banana and process until smooth.

3 Pour the mixture into glasses and decorate with slices of orange and whole strawberries on cocktail sticks.

raspberry & strawberry smoothie

ingredients

SERVES 2–4

55 g/2 oz raspberries

55 g/2 oz strawberries, halved

225 ml/8 fl oz crème fraîche

225 ml/8 fl oz milk

1 tsp almond essence (optional)

2–3 tbsp clear honey, to taste

method

1 Press the raspberries through a nylon sieve into a bowl using the back of a spoon. Discard the seeds in the sieve.

2 Put the raspberry purée, strawberries, crème fraîche, milk and almond essence (if using) into a food processor or blender and process until smooth and combined.

3 Pour the smoothie into chilled glasses, stir in honey to taste and serve.

melon & pineapple crush

ingredients

SERVES 2

100 ml/3^1/$_2$ fl oz pineapple juice

4 tbsp orange juice

125 g/4^1/$_2$ oz galia melon, cut into chunks

140 g/5 oz frozen pineapple chunks

4 ice cubes

slices of galia melon, to decorate

method

1 Pour the pineapple juice and orange juice into a food processor or blender and process gently until combined.

2 Add the melon, pineapple chunks and ice cubes and process until a slushy consistency has been reached.

3 Pour the mixture into glasses and decorate with slices of melon.

4 Serve at once.

bright eyes

ingredients

SERVES 1–2

100 ml/3¹/₂ fl oz boiling water

1 green tea sachet, or 1 tsp green tea

1 carrot

1 apple

small handful of flat-leaf parsley

sprigs of flat-leaf parsley, to garnish

method

1 Pour the boiling water onto the green tea and leave to stand for 4 minutes. Strain and cool slightly.

2 Process or blend together the carrot, apple and parsley. Stir the juice into the tea.

3 Pour into glasses and serve warm or cold, garnished with parsley sprigs.

fruit kefir

ingredients

SERVES 4

1 banana
115 g/4 oz strawberries, halved
225 ml/8 fl oz peach yogurt
2 tbsp clear honey
225 ml/8 fl oz apple juice, chilled

method

1 Peel the banana and slice it directly into a food processor or blender.

2 Add the strawberries, yogurt and honey and process until smooth. With the motor running, pour in the apple juice through the hole in the lid.

3 Pour into chilled glasses and serve.

banana, peach & strawberry smoothie

ingredients

SERVES 2

300 ml/10 fl oz full-fat milk or soya milk

2 tbsp natural yogurt

1 tbsp maple syrup

1/2 peeled and sliced banana

1/2 stoned, peeled and chopped peach

3 hulled strawberries

method

1 Put all the ingredients into a food processor or blender and process until combined and frothy.

2 Pour into glasses and serve immediately.

fruity refresher

ingredients

SERVES 1–2

$^1/_2$ peach

1 small apple

$^1/_2$ kiwi fruit

55 g/2 oz green grapes

200 g/7 oz honeydew melon flesh

slices of kiwi fruit, to garnish

method

1 Halve and stone the peach.

2 Process or blend together the peach, apple and kiwi fruit, then add the grapes and melon.

3 Stir the juice. Pour into glasses and decorate with the slices of kiwi fruit.

orchard fruit smoothie

ingredients

SERVES 2

1 ripe pear, peeled and quartered

1 apple, peeled and quartered

2 large red or dark plums, halved and stoned

4 ripe damsons, halved and stoned

200 ml// fl oz water

slices of apple or pear, to decorate

method

1 Put the pear, apple, plums, damsons and water into a small saucepan. Cover tightly, set over a medium heat and bring slowly to the boil. Take off the heat and allow to cool. Chill.

2 Put the fruit and water into a food processor or blender and process until smooth.

3 Pour into glasses, decorate with slices of apple or pear and serve.

red reviver

ingredients

SERVES 1–2

2 small beetroot

1 carrot

1 pear

$^1/_2$ lime

2.5-cm/1-inch piece of fresh ginger

method

1 Process or blend together the beetroot and carrot, then blend the pear, lime and ginger. Mix together.

2 Pour into glasses and serve.

pink zinger

ingredients

SERVES 1–2

1 pink grapefruit

1 orange

$1/2$ lemon

$1/2$ lime

slices of lime, to decorate

method

1 Peel the grapefruit, orange, lemon and lime, leaving on the white pith.

2 Process or blend together the grapefruit, orange, lemon and lime.

3 Pour into glasses and decorate with the slices of lime.

carrot & red pepper booster

ingredients

SERVES 2

250 ml/9 fl oz carrot juice

250 ml/9 fl oz tomato juice

2 large red peppers, deseeded and roughly chopped

1 tbsp lemon juice

freshly ground black pepper

method

1 Pour the carrot juice and tomato juice into a food processor or blender and process gently until combined.

2 Add the red peppers and lemon juice. Season with plenty of freshly ground black pepper and process until smooth.

3 Pour the mixture into glasses and serve.

revive

From time to time, everyone in the family can feel out of sorts – they may have had a nasty cold, been sleeping badly, be under pressure at work or school or simply have been so busy they have been skipping meals and surviving on unhealthy snacks. Smoothies are a great way of recharging the batteries, especially as the appetite tends to wane when you're not feeling yourself.

Most people know that oranges and other citrus fruits have high levels of vitamin C that help to ward off infections, but so, too, do tomatoes, peppers and kiwis. Like bananas, kiwis are also a good source of potassium, essential for regulating blood pressure, so smoothies made with these fruits can really help prevent you from blowing your top! Replenish essential minerals with tropical fruits and cleanse the system with apples and carrots. Beetroot is a great all-round pick-me-up and it's probably one of the world's best-kept secrets that it even relieves a hangover.

Growing older is a fact of life but smoothies are literally revitalizers as most fruits and vegetables contain antioxidants with anti-ageing properties. They can even help combat wrinkles and sagging skin. For example, berries, especially dark ones such as blackberries and blueberries, are great for restoring skin tone and, as a bonus, help prevent memory loss.

banana & strawberry smoothie

ingredients

SERVES 2

1 banana, sliced

85 g/3 oz fresh strawberries, hulled

150 g/5¹/₂ oz low-fat natural yogurt

method

1 Put the banana, strawberries and yogurt into a food processor or blender and process for a few seconds until smooth.

2 Pour into glasses and serve immediately.

papaya & banana smoothie

ingredients

SERVES 2

1 papaya
juice of 1 lime
1 large banana
350 ml/12 fl oz freshly squeezed orange juice
1/4 tsp ground ginger

method

1 Halve the papaya and scoop out and discard the grey-black seeds.
Scoop out the flesh and chop coarsely, then toss with the lime juice.
Peel and slice the banana.

2 Put the papaya, banana, orange juice and ginger into a food
processor or blender and process until thoroughly combined.

3 Pour into chilled glasses and serve.

detox special

ingredients

SERVES 2

1 mango
4 kiwi fruit
350 ml/12 fl oz pineapple juice
4 fresh mint leaves

method

1 Cut the mango into 2 thick slices as close to the stone as possible. Scoop out the flesh and chop coarsely. Cut off any flesh adhering to the stone. Peel the kiwi fruit with a sharp knife and chop the flesh.

2 Put the mango, kiwi fruit, pineapple juice and mint leaves into a food processor or blender and process until thoroughly combined.

3 Pour into chilled glasses and serve.

tropical smoothie

ingredients

SERVES 2

1 ripe papaya, peeled, stoned and chopped

$^1/_2$ fresh pineapple, peeled and chopped

150 ml/5 fl oz soya milk

300 ml/10 fl oz soya yogurt

chopped pineapple, to decorate

method

1 Place all the ingredients in a food processor or blender and process until smooth.

2 Pour into glasses, decorate with chopped pineapple and serve.

sunshine smoothie

ingredients

SERVES 1–2

2 nectarines

100 g/3^{1}/$_{2}$ oz green seedless grapes

100 g/3^{1}/$_{2}$ oz soya yogurt

^{1}/$_{2}$ tsp honey, preferably Manuka

1 tbsp sunflower seeds

method

1 Halve and stone the nectarines, then process or blend with the grapes.

2 Add the yogurt, honey and half the sunflower seeds and process until smooth.

3 Pour into glasses, sprinkle with the remaining sunflower seeds and serve.

cherry pink

ingredients

SERVES 1–2

350 g/12 oz dark sweet cherries

$1/2$ lime

1 apple

100 g/$3^1/2$ oz red grapes

40 g/$1^1/2$ oz soya yogurt

method

1 Stone the cherries. Peel the lime.

2 Process or blend together the apple, cherries, grapes and lime. Whisk in the yogurt.

3 Pour into glasses and serve.

blueberry dazzler

ingredients

SERVES 2

175 ml/6 fl oz apple juice
125 ml/4 fl oz natural yogurt
1 banana, sliced and frozen
175 g/6 oz frozen blueberries
whole fresh blueberries on cocktail sticks, to decorate

method

1 Pour the apple juice into a food processor or blender. Add the yogurt and process until smooth.

2 Add the banana and half of the blueberries and process well, then add the remaining blueberries and process until smooth.

3 Pour the mixture into tall glasses.

4 Decorate with whole fresh blueberries on cocktail sticks and serve.

pear & raspberry delight

ingredients

SERVES 2

2 large ripe Conference pears

125 g/4$^{1}/_{2}$ oz frozen raspberries

200 ml/7 fl oz ice-cold water

honey, to taste

raspberries on cocktail sticks, to decorate

method

1 Peel and quarter the pears, removing the cores. Put into a food processor or blender with the raspberries and water and process until smooth.

2 Taste and sweeten with honey if the raspberries are a little sharp.

3 Pour into glasses, decorate with whole raspberries on cocktail sticks and serve.

apricot & orange smoothie

ingredients

SERVES 2

125 g/4¹/₂ oz dried apricots
250 ml/9 fl oz boiling water
juice of 4 medium oranges
2 tbsp natural yogurt
1 tsp soft dark brown sugar

method

1 Put the apricots in a bowl and pour the boiling water over them. Leave to soak overnight.

2 In the morning, put the apricots and their soaking water into a food processor or blender and process until puréed. Add the orange juice to the apricots in the food processor, and process until combined.

3 Pour into glasses and top with the tablespoons of yogurt and the brown sugar.

berry booster

ingredients

SERVES 1

25 g/1 oz blueberries

85 g/3 oz raspberries, thawed if frozen

1 tsp clear honey

200 ml/7 fl oz live or bio yogurt

about 1 heaped tbsp crushed ice

1 tbsp sesame seeds

method

1 Put the blueberries into a food processor or blender and process for 1 minute.

2 Add the raspberries, honey and yogurt and process for a further minute.

3 Add the ice and sesame seeds and process again for a further minute.

4 Pour into a glass and serve immediately.

black & blue

ingredients

SERVES 2

125 g/4^1/$_2$ oz cultivated blackberries
125 g/4^1/$_2$ oz blueberries
100 ml/3^1/$_2$ fl oz ice-cold water
150 ml/5 fl oz natural yogurt

method

1 Put the blackberries, blueberries, water and yogurt into a food processor or blender and process until smooth.

2 Pour into glasses and serve.

apple, carrot & cucumber juice

ingredients

SERVES 1

1 apple, unpeeled, cored and chopped

1 carrot, peeled and chopped

$^{1}/_{2}$ cucumber, chopped

pieces of carrot, cucumber and apple on a cocktail stick, to decorate

method

1 Place the chopped apple, carrot and cucumber in a food processor or blender and process.

2 Pour into a glass, decorate with the fruit on a cocktail stick and serve.

guava goodness

ingredients

SERVES 2

400 g/14 oz canned guavas, drained

250 ml/9 fl oz ice-cold milk

method

1 Place the guavas in a food processor or blender and pour in the milk. Process until well blended.

2 Strain into glasses to remove the hard seeds. Serve.

24 carrot

ingredients

SERVES 2

handful of cracked ice

2 carrots, coarsely chopped

115 g/4 oz canned pineapple pieces in juice, drained

175 ml/6 fl oz pineapple juice, chilled

strips of cucumber, to decorate

method

1 Put the ice into a food processsor or blender, add the carrots, pineapple pieces and pineapple juice and process until slushy.

2 Pour into chilled glasses and decorate with strips of cucumber.

mint & cucumber refresher

ingredients

SERVES 1

few sprigs of mint
1 tsp caster sugar
juice of 1 lime
2 cm/³/₄ in piece cucumber, thinly sliced
your favourite sparkling water, chilled
ice cubes

method

1 Chop a few mint leaves and mix with the sugar.

2 Rub a little lime juice round the rim of a pretty glass and dip it in the minted sugar. Leave to dry.

3 Mix the rest of the lime juice, cucumber and mint – some chopped and some whole – in a jug and chill.

4 To serve, pour the lime and cucumber into the prepared glass and top up to taste with chilled sparkling water and ice cubes.

apple & celery revitalizer

ingredients

SERVES 2

1 eating apple, peeled, cored and diced

115 g/4 oz celery, chopped

600 ml/1 pint milk

pinch of sugar (optional)

salt (optional)

strips of celery, to decorate

method

1 Put the apple, celery and milk into a food processor or blender and process until thoroughly combined.

2 Stir in a pinch of sugar and some salt, if using.

3 Pour into chilled glasses, decorate with strips of celery and serve.

the reviver

ingredients

SERVES 1–2

$^1/_2$ galia melon

3 celery sticks

125 g/4$^1/_2$ oz blackberries

1 kiwi fruit, peeled

method

1 Peel the melon and cut into chunks.

2 Put the chunks into a food processor or blender with 1 celery stick, the blackberries and the kiwi fruit.

3 Process or blend all the ingredients together, then pour into glasses and serve with the remaining celery sticks to stir.

rapid recharge

ingredients

SERVES 1–2

1 small courgette

1 celery stick

40 g/1 $^1/_2$ oz baby leaf spinach

40 g/1 $^1/_2$ oz alfalfa sprouts

2 apples, peeled and cored

1 tsp alfalfa sprouts, to decorate

method

1 Top and tail the courgette and place in a food processor or blender with the celery. Add the spinach and the alfalfa, then the apples.

2 Process or blend all the ingredients together, then pour into glasses.

3 Decorate with a few alfalfa sprouts and serve.

red pepper reactor

ingredients

SERVES 2

250 ml/9 fl oz carrot juice

250 ml/9 fl oz tomato juice

2 large red peppers, deseeded and roughly chopped

1 tbsp lemon juice

freshly ground black pepper

strips of shredded carrot, to decorate

method

1 Pour the carrot juice and tomato juice into a food processor or blender and process gently until combined.

2 Add the red peppers and lemon juice. Season with plenty of freshly ground black pepper and process until smooth.

3 Pour the mixture into glasses, decorate with the strips of shredded carrot and serve.

on the beat

ingredients

SERVES 2

175 g/6 oz cooked beetroot, chopped

125 ml/4 fl oz orange juice, chilled

5 tbsp natural yogurt, chilled

150 ml/5 fl oz still mineral water, chilled

salt

slices of orange, to decorate

method

1 Put the beetroot, orange juice, yogurt and water into a food processor or blender and season to taste with salt.

2 Process until smooth, then pour into chilled glasses and serve, decorated with slices of orange.

refresh

On a hot summer's day or after a burst of vigorous exercise, a long, thirst-quenching cooler is just what's needed rather than a creamy and substantial smoothie. Fortunately, there are fruits so full of juice and with such naturally refreshing flavours that they fit the bill exactly. Apart from the citrus family, watermelon, pineapple, mango and pomegranate instantly spring to mind. Sweet enough to delight the taste buds without being sticky or cloying, they mix and match into deliciously fresh-flavoured summer drinks.

Sometimes whole fruits are combined with pure juice for instant rehydration, but this does not in any way detract from the health-giving, restorative properties of refresher smoothies. A baking hot day can leave you feeling limp and lethargic so it's important to re-establish the body's balance as well as replace the fluid lost through sweating. Equally, a restorative smoothie following an energetic session of exercise will help maintain that satisfying feeling of invigoration. Fruits rich in calcium and magnesium, such as oranges and apricots, stimulate cell repair, while apples, mangoes and passion fruit help replace lost energy.

It's worth remembering to put fruit juice and glasses in the refrigerator to chill in advance so that when you mix your drink it is pleasantly cool. Adding ice cubes would work too, of course, but would also dilute the flavour.

raspberry & apple quencher

ingredients

SERVES 2

8 ice cubes, crushed

2 tbsp raspberry syrup

500 ml/18 fl oz chilled apple juice

pieces of apple and whole raspberries on cocktail sticks, to decorate

method

1 Divide the crushed ice between two glasses and pour over the raspberry syrup.

2 Top up each glass with chilled apple juice and stir well.

3 Decorate with the pieces of apple and the whole raspberries on cocktail sticks and serve.

watermelon whizz

ingredients

SERVES 2

wedge of watermelon, weighing about 350 g/12 oz

ice cubes

slices of watermelon, to decorate

method

1 Cut the rind off the watermelon. Chop the watermelon into chunks, discarding any seeds.

2 Put the watermelon chunks into a food processor or blender and process until smooth.

3 Place the ice cubes in the glasses. Pour the watermelon mixture over the ice and serve decorated with the slices of watermelon.

perky pineapple

ingredients

SERVES 4

handful of cracked ice

2 bananas

225 ml/8 fl oz pineapple juice, chilled

125 ml/4 fl oz lime juice

slices of pineapple, to decorate

method

1 Put the cracked ice into a food processor or blender. Peel the bananas and slice directly into the processor. Add the pineapple and lime juices and process until smooth.

2 Pour into chilled glasses, decorate with slices of pineapple and serve.

melon & mango tango

ingredients

SERVES 2

1 cantaloupe melon, halved and deseeded
600 ml/1 pint mango juice
2 tbsp fresh orange juice
slices of orange, to decorate

method

1 Scoop out the melon flesh with a spoon straight into a food processor or blender. Add the mango and orange juices and process until smooth.

2 Pour into chilled glasses, decorate with slices of orange and serve.

blueberry nectar

ingredients

SERVES 1–2

1 pear
150 g/5^1/$_2$ oz blueberries
100 g/3^1/$_2$ oz soya yogurt
^{1}/$_2$ tsp agave syrup
2 tsp toasted flaked almonds

method

1 Put the pear and blueberries into a food processor or blender.

2 Add the yogurt and agave syrup and blend until smooth and bubbly.

3 Pour into glasses, sprinkle with the almonds and serve.

fresh & fruity

ingredients

SERVES 1–2

$^1/_2$ small pineapple

85 g/3 oz blackberries

85 g/3 oz blueberries

1 tsp goji berries, roughly chopped, to decorate

method

1 Cut the pineapple into chunks and process or blend with the blackberries and blueberries.

2 Pour into glasses and sprinkle with the chopped goji berries.

apricot buzz

ingredients

SERVES 1–2

6 apricots

1 orange

1 fresh lemon grass stalk

2-cm/³/4-inch piece of fresh ginger

method

1 Halve and stone the apricots. Peel the orange, leaving some of the white pith. Cut the lemon grass into chunks.

2 Place the apricots, orange, lemon grass and ginger in a food processor or blender and blend all the ingredients together.

3 Pour into glasses and serve.

watermelon sunset

ingredients

SERVES 4

1 watermelon, halved
6 tbsp fresh ruby grapefruit juice
6 tbsp fresh orange juice
dash of lime juice
slices of watermelon, to decorate

method

1 Deseed the watermelon if you are unable to find a seedless one. Scoop the flesh into a food processor or blender and add the grapefruit juice, orange juice and a dash of lime juice.

2 Process until smooth, pour into chilled glasses, decorate with slices of watermelon and serve.

apple cooler

ingredients

SERVES 2

2 ripe apples, peeled and roughly chopped

55 g/2 oz strawberries, hulled

juice of 4 oranges

sugar, to taste

slices of apple, to decorate

method

1 Put the apples, strawberries and orange juice into a food processor or blender and process until smooth.

2 Taste and sweeten with sugar if necessary.

3 Decorate with slices of apple and serve at once.

lemon surprise

ingredients

SERVES 2

juice of 1 lemon
1 tbsp chopped fresh parsley
425 ml/15 fl oz sparkling mineral water
2–3 tsp sugar

method

1 Put the lemon juice, parsley and mineral water into a food processor or blender and process on low speed until combined.

2 Switch to high speed, add the sugar through the feeder tube and process for 30 seconds more.

3 Pour into chilled glasses and serve.

maidenly mimosa

ingredients

SERVES 2

175 ml/6 fl oz freshly squeezed orange juice
175 ml/6 fl oz sparkling white grape juice

method

1 Divide the orange juice between 2 chilled wine glasses or champagne flutes.

2 Top up with the grape juice and serve.

pomegranate passion

ingredients

SERVES 2

2 ripe pomegranates

1 passion fruit

1 tbsp clear honey

2 glasses full of crushed ice

method

1 Cut the pomegranates in half and extract the juice with an old-fashioned lemon squeezer.

2 Halve the passion fruit and sieve the pulp into a small bowl. Mix in the pomegranate juice and honey.

3 Pour over the crushed ice and serve.

passionate juice fizz

ingredients

SERVES 1–2

1 pomegranate

1/2 small orange

4 passion fruits

100–125 ml/3¹/₂–4¹/₂ fl oz sparkling mineral water

method

1 Peel the rind from the pomegranate and peel the orange, leaving on the white pith. Scoop the flesh from the passion fruits.

2 Process or blend the pomegranate with the orange and pulp from 3 passion fruits.

3 Pour into glasses and stir in the remaining passion fruit pulp. Top up with the mineral water and serve.

strawberry & pineapple refresher

ingredients

SERVES 2

150 g/5^1/$_2$ oz frozen strawberries

300 ml/10 fl oz long-life pineapple juice

1 tbsp caster sugar

wedges of pineapple, to decorate

method

1 Put the strawberries, pineapple juice and caster sugar into a food processor or blender and process until smooth.

2 Pour into glasses, decorate with wedges of pineapple and serve.

black grape fizz

ingredients

SERVES 2

125 g/4^1/$_2$ oz black grapes, deseeded or seedless
200 ml/7 fl oz sparkling mineral water
2 large scoops of lemon sorbet
slices of lime, to decorate

method

1 Put the grapes, mineral water and lemon sorbet into a food processor or blender and process until smooth.

2 Pour into glasses and decorate with slices of lime. Serve immediately.

homemade lemonade

ingredients

SERVES 2

150 ml/5 fl oz water

6 tbsp sugar

1 tsp grated lemon rind

125 ml/4 fl oz lemon juice

6 ice cubes

sparkling water, to serve

granulated sugar and slices of lemon, to decorate

method

1 Put the water, sugar and grated lemon rind into a small saucepan and bring to the boil, stirring constantly. Continue to boil, stirring, for 5 minutes.

2 Remove from the heat and leave to cool to room temperature. Stir in the lemon juice, then transfer to a jug, cover with clingfilm and chill in the refrigerator for at least 2 hours.

3 When the lemonade has almost finished chilling, take two glasses and rub the rims with a wedge of lemon, then dip them in granulated sugar to frost. Put the ice cubes into the glasses.

4 Remove the lemon syrup from the refrigerator, pour it over the ice and top up with sparkling water. The ratio should be one part lemon syrup to three parts sparkling water. Stir well to mix, decorate with sugar and slices of fresh lemon and serve.

soothe

Life is so hectic nowadays that even when we do have some time to ourselves, it is often difficult to relax and unwind. Most of us have known nights when we fall exhausted into bed but the mind keeps on going, churning over the day's concerns and worrying about tomorrow's. Let go with a soothing smoothie, releasing the tension and calming both mind and body, confident that every restorative sip is doing you good. It's not just healthier than a glass of wine – alcohol depletes the body's supplies of important vitamins and minerals – but more effective too.

These smoothies do far more than just replace the energy used up during the day. They are great stress busters in their own right. Research has shown that a pressurized lifestyle actually robs the body of essential vitamins and minerals, so it is important to replace these. In addition, an increased intake of vitamin C reduces the levels of stress hormones in the blood and actually lifts the spirits. A smoothie made with citrus fruits, cantaloupe melon, berries or kiwis, for example, is an easy way to achieve this and more fun to swallow than supplements. Its natural sweetness will help you get a good night's sleep, too.

sunrise crush

ingredients

SERVES 4

1 medium ripe pineapple
5 oranges, halved
ice cubes, to serve

method

1 Slice the bottom off the pineapple and stand the pineapple upright on a board. Remove the spiky skin then cut into six long pieces.

2 Purée the pineapple in a food processor or blender.

3 Squeeze the oranges, then mix the orange and pineapple juices together in a jug. Pour the juice into 4 glasses. Top with ice cubes.

summer fruit slush

ingredients

SERVES 2

4 tbsp orange juice

1 tbsp lime juice

100 ml/3½ fl oz sparkling water

350 g/12 oz frozen summer fruits (such as blueberries, raspberries, blackberries and strawberries)

4 ice cubes

method

1 Pour the orange juice, lime juice and sparkling water into a food processor or blender and process gently until combined.

2 Add the summer fruits and ice cubes and process until a slushy consistency has been reached.

3 Pour the mixture into glasses and serve.

forest fruit smoothie

ingredients

SERVES 2

350 ml/12 fl oz orange juice

1 banana, sliced and frozen

450 g/1 lb frozen forest fruits (such as blueberries, raspberries and blackberries)

slices of orange, to decorate

method

1 Pour the orange juice into a food processor or blender. Add the banana and half of the forest fruits and process until smooth.

2 Add the remaining forest fruits and process until smooth.

3 Pour the mixture into glasses and decorate the rims with slices of orange.

passionate magic

ingredients

SERVES 1–2

2 peaches
140 g/5 oz red grapes
115 g/4 oz strawberries
1 passion fruit
seeds from $1/2$ vanilla pod

method

1 Halve and stone the peaches and process or blend with the grapes and strawberries.

2 Halve the passion fruit and scoop out the flesh, scrape the seeds from the vanilla pod and stir both into the juice.

3 Pour into glasses and serve.

mango & orange smoothie

ingredients

SERVES 2

1 large ripe mango
juice of 2 medium oranges
3 scoops of mango sorbet
strips of orange zest, to decorate

method

1 Place the mango on a chopping board and cut lengthways through the flesh as close to the large flat central stone as possible. Turn it over and do the same thing on the other side of the stone. Remove the peel and roughly chop the flesh before placing in a food processor or blender.

2 Add the orange juice and sorbet and process until smooth.

3 Serve at once, decorated with strips of orange zest.

honeydew

ingredients

SERVES 2

250 g/9 oz honeydew melon

300 ml/10 fl oz sparkling mineral water

2 tbsp clear honey

redcurrant clusters, to decorate

method

1 Cut the rind off the melon. Chop the melon into chunks, discarding any seeds.

2 Put into a food processor or blender with the water and honey and process until smooth.

3 Pour into glasses and decorate with clusters of redcurrants.

melon refresher

ingredients

SERVES 2

250 ml/9 fl oz natural yogurt

100 g/3$\frac{1}{2}$ oz galia melon, cut into chunks

100 g/3$\frac{1}{2}$ oz cantaloupe melon, cut into chunks

100 g/3$\frac{1}{2}$ oz watermelon, cut into chunks

6 ice cubes

wedges of melon, to decorate

method

1 Pour the yogurt into a food processor or blender. Add the galia melon chunks and process until smooth.

2 Add the cantaloupe and watermelon chunks along with the ice cubes and process until smooth.

3 Pour the mixture into glasses and decorate with wedges of melon.

4 Serve at once.

cherry sour

ingredients

SERVES 2

250 g/9 oz bottled stoned morello cherries

150 ml/5 fl oz Greek yogurt

sugar, to taste

cherries on cocktail sticks, to decorate

method

1 Put the cherries with their bottling liquid into a food processor or blender with the yogurt and process until smooth.

2 Taste and sweeten with sugar if necessary.

3 Pour into glasses and serve. Decorate with cherries on a cocktail stick.

cherry kiss

ingredients

SERVES 2

8 ice cubes, crushed

2 tbsp cherry syrup

500 ml/18 fl oz sparkling water

maraschino cherries on long swizzle sticks, to decorate

method

1 Divide the crushed ice between two glasses and pour over the cherry syrup.

2 Top up each glass with sparkling water. Decorate with the maraschino cherries on long swizzle sticks and serve.

kiwi cooler

ingredients

SERVES 2

4 ripe kiwi fruit, peeled and quartered

200 ml/7 fl oz traditional sparkling lemonade

2 large scoops of ice cream or sorbet, to decorate

method

1 Put the kiwi fruit and lemonade into a food processor or blender and process until smooth.

2 Pour into glasses and top with scoops of ice cream or sorbet.

3 Serve at once.

white grape elderflower foam

ingredients

SERVES 2

125 g/4$^{1}/_{2}$ oz white grapes, deseeded or seedless

200 ml/7 fl oz sparkling mineral water

2 large scoops of frozen yogurt (plain)

·1$^{1}/_{2}$ tbsp elderflower cordial

white grapes, to decorate

method

1 Put the grapes, mineral water, frozen yogurt and elderflower cordial into a food processor or blender and process until smooth.

2 Pour into glasses, add a few grapes and serve immediately.

kiwi juice

ingredients

SERVES 1–2

1 kiwi fruit

1 apple

115 g/4 oz seedless white grapes

method

1 Process or blend the kiwi fruit and apple, then the grapes.

2 Pour into glasses and serve just as it is, or pour over ice.

pineapple tango

ingredients

SERVES 2

125 ml/4 fl oz pineapple juice

juice of 1 lemon

100 ml/3^1/$_2$ fl oz water

3 tbsp brown sugar

175 ml/6 fl oz natural yogurt

1 peach, cut into chunks and frozen

100 g/3^1/$_2$ oz frozen pineapple chunks

slices of fresh pineapple, to decorate

method

1 Pour the pineapple juice, lemon juice and water into a food processor or blender. Add the sugar and yogurt and process until blended.

2 Add the peach and pineapple chunks and process until smooth.

3 Pour the mixture into glasses and decorate the rims with slices of fresh pineapple.

4 Serve at once.

elderflower & pear smoothie

ingredients

SERVES 2

4 small firm pears

2 heads of elderflowers, freshly picked (or a dash of cordial)

1 strip of lemon zest

1 tbsp soft brown sugar

4 tbsp water

200 ml/7 fl oz semi-skimmed milk

langues de chat biscuits, to serve

method

1 Peel and quarter the pears, discarding the cores. Place in a saucepan with the elderflowers, a strip of lemon zest, the sugar and water. Cover tightly and simmer until the pears are very soft. Allow to cool.

2 Discard the elderflowers and lemon zest. Put the pears, cooking liquid and milk into a food processor or blender and process until smooth.

3 Serve immediately with langues de chat biscuits.

cold comforter

ingredients

SERVES 1–2

1 white grapefruit

1 orange

1 kiwi fruit

15 drops echinacea tincture

thinly pared twists of orange zest, to decorate

method

1 Peel the grapefruit and orange, leaving on some of the white pith.

2 Process or blend the grapefruit, orange and kiwi fruit together. Stir in the echinacea drops and pour into glasses.

3 Add a twist of orange zest to each and serve.

one for the girls

ingredients

SERVES 1–2

1 apple

1 large carrot

1 celery stick

$1/2$ fennel bulb

$1/2$ tsp linseeds (flax seeds)

method

1 Process or blend the apple, carrot, celery and fennel together.

2 Pour into glasses and sprinkle with linseeds to serve.

spiced fruit boost

ingredients

SERVES 1–2

$^1/_2$ lemon

2 apples

85 g/3 oz stoned prunes

2 pears

freshly grated nutmeg, to decorate

method

1 Peel the lemon, leaving on a layer of white pith.

2 Process or blend the apples, lemon, prunes and pears together.

3 Pour into glasses, sprinkle with grated nutmeg and serve.

green goddess

ingredients

SERVES 1–2

$^{1}/_{2}$ galia melon

85 g/3 oz baby leaf spinach

2 large sprigs mint, plus extra to decorate

2 large sprigs flat-leaf parsley

method

1 Cut the outer hard rind from the melon, leaving the inner green layer, and cut into chunks.

2 Pack half into a food processor or blender, pack the spinach and herbs in firmly, then top with the remaining melon.

3 Process or blend the ingredients, then pour into glasses over ice. Add a sprig of mint to each and serve.

blood orange sparkler

ingredients

SERVES 2

250 ml/9 fl oz blood (ruby) orange juice
100 g/3¹/₂ oz strawberries
100 g/3¹/₂ oz raspberries
50 ml/2 fl oz sparkling mineral water

method

1 Put the blood orange juice, strawberries, raspberries and mineral water into a food processor or blender and process until smooth. Sieve the mixture to remove the pips, if preferred.

2 Pour into glasses and serve.

hot blackcurrant toddy

ingredients

SERVES 1–2

1 apple
200 g/7 oz blackcurrants
1 tsp set honey, preferably Manuka
100 ml/3$\frac{1}{2}$ fl oz boiling water

method

1 Process or blend the apple with the blackcurrants.

2 Add the honey to the boiling water and stir to dissolve, then stir in the juice.

3 Pour into glasses and serve immediately.

bliss

We all need a treat now and again and an occasional moment of self-indulgence is good for the soul. These smoothies allow you to yield to the enticing lure of your favourite naughty pleasure once in a while without going completely over the top.

Of course, fruit smoothies still feature but here they are combined in deliciously rich and creamy mixtures or mouthwatering medleys of luscious sweetness. Everyone's top temptation – chocolate – takes a starring role in several fabulous concoctions, sometimes sharing centre stage with that other delicious addiction – coffee.

Not all these blissful smoothies are quite such guilty pleasures. Rather, they are unusual drinks that hit the spot when you feel like something a little different and can't think exactly what. If you want to spice up a dull evening, don't head for the cocktail shaker – set off for the blender instead and try some tasty piquant treats with ginger or peppermint. Set a tropical mood with a velvety coconut smoothie, or a garden party atmosphere with strawberries and cream.

Bliss is not just for adults – the younger members of the family will love these special smoothies too. They're probably not for everyday drinking but would be the perfect choice for a birthday party or other special occasion.

strawberries & cream milkshake

ingredients

SERVES 2

150 g/5^1/$_2$ oz frozen strawberries
100 ml/3^1/$_2$ fl oz single cream
200 ml/7 fl oz cold milk
1 tbsp caster sugar
mint leaves, to decorate

method

1 Put the strawberries, cream, milk and caster sugar into a food processor or blender and process until smooth.

2 Pour into glasses and serve decorated with mint leaves.

chocolate milkshake

ingredients

SERVES 2

150 ml/5 fl oz milk

2 tbsp chocolate syrup

400 g/14 oz chocolate ice cream

grated chocolate, to decorate

method

1 Pour the milk and chocolate syrup into a food processor or blender and process gently until combined.

2 Add the chocolate ice cream and process until smooth. Pour the mixture into tall glasses and scatter the grated chocolate over the shakes.

3 Serve at once.

spiced banana milkshake

ingredients

SERVES 2

300 ml/10 fl oz milk

$^1/_2$ tsp mixed spice

150 g/5$^1/_2$ oz banana ice cream

2 bananas, sliced and frozen

pinch of mixed spice, to decorate

method

1 Pour the milk into a food processor or blender and add the mixed spice. Add half of the banana ice cream and process gently until combined, then add the remaining ice cream and process until well blended.

2 When the mixture is well combined, add the bananas and process until smooth.

3 Pour the mixture into glasses, add a pinch of mixed spice to decorate and serve.

perfect plum shake

ingredients

SERVES 2

250 g/9 oz ripe plums, stoned

200 ml/7 fl oz water

1 tbsp golden granulated sugar

4 scoops of frozen yogurt (plain) or ice cream

plums, cut in half, to decorate

2 Italian almond or pistachio biscotti, crumbled, to serve

method

1 Put the plums, water and sugar into a small saucepan. Cover tightly and simmer for about 15 minutes, until the plums have split and are very soft. Allow to cool.

2 Strain off the liquid into a food processor or blender and add the frozen yogurt or ice cream. Process until smooth and frothy.

3 Pour into glasses and decorate the rims with halved plums. Sprinkle with the crumbled biscotti and serve.

creamy maple shake

ingredients

SERVES 2

150 ml/5 fl oz milk

2 tbsp maple syrup

400 g/14 oz vanilla ice cream

1 tbsp almond essence

chopped almonds, to decorate

method

1 Pour the milk and maple syrup into a food processor or blender and process gently until combined.

2 Add the ice cream and almond essence and process until smooth.

3 Pour the mixture into glasses, scatter the chopped nuts over the shakes and serve.

kiwi & lime shake

ingredients

SERVES 2

150 ml/5 fl oz milk

juice of 2 limes

2 kiwi fruits, chopped

1 tbsp sugar

400 g/14 oz vanilla ice cream

slices of kiwi fruit and strips of lime peel, to decorate

method

1 Pour the milk and lime juice into a food processor or blender and process gently until combined.

2 Add the kiwi fruit and sugar and process gently, then add the ice cream and process until smooth.

3 Pour the mixture into glasses and decorate with slices of kiwi fruit and strips of lime peel.

4 Serve at once.

peach & orange milkshake

ingredients

SERVES 2

100 ml/3¹/₂ fl oz milk
125 ml/4 fl oz peach yogurt
100 ml/3¹/₂ fl oz orange juice
225 g/8 oz canned peach slices, drained
6 ice cubes

method

1 Pour the milk, yogurt and orange juice into a food processor or blender and process gently until combined.

2 Add the peach slices and ice cubes and process until smooth. Pour the mixture into glasses.

smooth nectarine shake

ingredients

SERVES 2

250 ml/9 fl oz milk

350 g/12 oz lemon sorbet

1 ripe mango, stoned, peeled and diced

2 ripe nectarines, stoned and diced

thin wedges of nectarine, to decorate

method

1 Pour the milk into a food processor or blender, add half of the lemon sorbet and process gently until combined. Add the remaining sorbet and process until smooth.

2 When the mixture is thoroughly blended, gradually add the mango and nectarines and process until smooth.

3 Pour the mixture into glasses, decorate with thin wedges of nectarine and serve.

pink ginger shake

ingredients

SERVES 1–2

200 g/7 oz pink forced rhubarb

1 orange

2-cm/³/4-inch piece fresh ginger

50 ml/2 fl oz soya milk

pinch of ground ginger, to decorate

method

1 Trim the rhubarb and cut into chunks. Peel the orange, leaving some of the white pith.

2 Process or blend the rhubarb, orange and ginger. Add the milk and blend to mix.

3 Pour into glasses, sprinkle with ginger and serve.

tropical storm

ingredients

SERVES 2

250 ml/9 fl oz milk

50 ml/2 fl oz coconut milk

150 g/5½ oz vanilla ice cream

2 bananas, sliced and frozen

200 g/7 oz canned pineapple chunks, drained

1 papaya, deseeded and diced

grated coconut, to decorate

method

1 Pour the milk and coconut milk into a food processor or blender and process gently until combined. Add half of the ice cream and process gently, then add the remaining ice cream and process until smooth.

2 Add the bananas and process well, then add the pineapple chunks and papaya and process until smooth.

3 Pour the mixture into glasses and scatter the grated coconut over the top and serve.

plum fluff

ingredients

SERVES 2

4 medium ripe plums, stoned

200 ml/7 fl oz ice-cold milk

2 scoops of luxury vanilla ice cream

crumbly oat biscuits, to serve

method

1 Put the plums, milk and ice cream into a food processor or blender and process until smooth and frothy.

2 Pour into glasses and serve at once with crumbly oat biscuits.

peach bliss

ingredients

SERVES 2

175 ml/6 fl oz milk
225 g/8 oz canned peach slices, drained
2 fresh apricots, chopped
400 g/14 oz fresh strawberries, hulled and sliced
2 bananas, sliced and frozen
slices of nectarine, strawberries and banana on cocktail sticks, to decorate

method

1 Pour the milk into a food processor or blender. Add the peach slices and process gently until combined. Add the apricots and process gently until combined.

2 Add the strawberries and banana slices and process until smooth.

3 Pour the mixture into glasses and decorate with the fruit speared on a cocktail stick.

4 Serve at once.

black & white smoothie

ingredients

SERVES 2

150 g/5¹/₂ oz black cherries

3 large scoops of luxury white chocolate ice cream

150 ml/5 fl oz milk

method

1 Halve and stone the black cherries. Put these into a food processor or blender and process until puréed.

2 Add the ice cream and milk and process briefly to mix well.

3 Pour into glasses and serve.

coconut cream

ingredients

SERVES 2

350 ml/12 fl oz pineapple juice

90 ml/3$^1/_4$ fl oz coconut milk

150 g/5$^1/_2$ oz vanilla ice cream

140 g/5 oz frozen pineapple chunks

2 tbsp grated fresh coconut, to decorate

2 scooped-out coconut shells, to serve (optional)

method

1 Pour the pineapple juice and coconut milk into a food processor or blender. Add the ice cream and process until smooth.

2 Add the pineapple chunks and process until smooth.

3 Pour the mixture into scooped-out coconut shells, or glasses, and decorate with grated fresh coconut.

peppermint refresher

ingredients

SERVES 2

150 ml/5 fl oz milk

2 tbsp peppermint syrup

400 g/14 oz peppermint ice cream

sprigs of fresh mint, to decorate

method

1 Pour the milk and peppermint syrup into a food processor or blender and process gently until combined.

2 Add the peppermint ice cream and process until smooth.

3 Pour the mixture into glasses and decorate with sprigs of fresh mint.

midsummer smoothie

ingredients

SERVES 2

1 ripe passion fruit

115 g/4 oz strawberries

115 g/4 oz raspberries

55 g/2 oz blueberries

150 ml/5 fl oz semi-skimmed milk

vanilla and strawberry ice cream, to decorate

method

1 Scoop out the passion fruit pulp. Place all the fruits in a food processor or blender and process for 1 minute. Add the milk and process again.

2 Pour into glasses and serve with a scoop of vanilla and strawberry ice cream on top of each.

iced coffee & chocolate crush

ingredients

SERVES 2

400 ml/14 fl oz milk

200 ml/7 fl oz coffee syrup

100 ml/3^1/$_2$ fl oz peppermint syrup

1 tbsp chopped fresh mint leaves

4 ice cubes

grated chocolate and sprigs of fresh mint, to decorate

method

1 Pour the milk, coffee syrup and peppermint syrup into a food processor or blender and process gently until combined.

2 Add the mint and ice cubes and process until a slushy consistency has been reached.

3 Pour the mixture into glasses. Scatter over the grated chocolate and the sprigs of fresh mint and serve.

mocha cream

ingredients

SERVES 2

200 ml/7 fl oz milk

50 ml/2 fl oz single cream

1 tbsp brown sugar

2 tbsp cocoa powder

1 tbsp coffee syrup or instant coffee powder

6 ice cubes

whipped cream and grated chocolate, to decorate

method

1 Put the milk, cream and sugar into a food processor or blender and process gently until combined.

2 Add the cocoa powder and coffee syrup and process well, then add the ice cubes and process until smooth.

3 Pour the mixture into glasses. Top with whipped cream, scatter the grated chocolate over the drinks and serve.

coffee banana cooler

ingredients

SERVES 2

300 ml/10 fl oz milk
4 tbsp instant coffee powder
150 g/5^1/$_2$ oz vanilla ice cream
2 bananas, sliced and frozen

method

1 Pour the milk into a food processor or blender, add the coffee powder and process gently until combined. Add half of the vanilla ice cream and process gently, then add the remaining ice cream and process until well combined.

2 When the mixture is thoroughly blended, add the bananas and process until smooth.

3 Pour the mixture into glasses and serve.

fig & maple melter

ingredients

SERVES 2

350 ml/12 fl oz hazelnut yogurt

2 tbsp freshly squeezed orange juice

4 tbsp maple syrup

8 large fresh figs, chopped

6 ice cubes

toasted chopped hazelnuts, to decorate

method

1 Pour the yogurt, orange juice and maple syrup into a food processor or blender and process gently until combined.

2 Add the figs and ice cubes and process until smooth.

3 Pour the mixture into glasses and scatter over some toasted chopped hazelnuts.

4 Serve at once.

apples
  apple & celery revitalizer 80
  apple, carrot & cucumber
    juice 72
  apple cooler 108
  bright eyes 32
  fruit kefir 34
  fruity refresher 38
  kiwi juice 148
  one for the girls 156
  orchard fruit smoothie 40
  rapid recharge 84
  raspberry & apple
    quencher 92
  spiced fruit boost 158
apricots
  apricot buzz 104
  apricot & orange smoothie 66
  peach bliss 190

bananas
  banana breakfast shake 12
  banana, peach & strawberry
    smoothie 36
  banana & strawberry
    smoothie 52
  breakfast smoothie 8
  coffee banana cooler 204
  papaya & banana smoothie 54
  peach bliss 190
  perky pineapple 96
  spiced banana milkshake 172
  tropical storm 186
beetroot
  on the beet 88
  red reviver 42
blackberries
  black & blue 70
  forest fruit smoothie 130
  fresh & fruity 102
  the reviver 82
  summer fruit slush 128
blackcurrants
  hot blackcurrant toddy 164
blueberries
  berry booster 68
  berry brightener 20
  black & blue 70
  blueberry dazzler 62
  blueberry nectar 100
  blueberry thrill 22
  forest fruit smoothie 130
  fresh & fruity 102
  midsummer smoothie 198
  summer fruit slush 128

carrots
  24 carrot 76
  apple, carrot & cucumber
    juice 72
  bright eyes 32
  carrot & red pepper booster 48
  one for the girls 156
  red pepper reactor 86
  rise & shine juice 10
celery
  apple & celery revitalizer 80
  one for the girls 156
  rapid recharge 84

the reviver 82
cherries
  black & white smoothie 192
  cherry kiss 142
  cherry pink 60
  cherry sour 140
chocolate milkshake 170
coconut
  coconut cream 194
  tropical storm 186
  tropical watermelon
    smoothie 24
coffee
  coffee banana cooler 204
  iced coffee & chocolate
    crush 200
  mocha cream 202
courgette: rapid recharge 84
cranberries
  berry brightener 20
cucumber
  apple, carrot & cucumber
    juice 72
  mint & cucumber refresher 78

damsons: orchard fruit
  smoothie 40

elderflowers
  elderflower & pear
    smoothie 152
  white grape elderflower
    foam 146

fig & maple melter 206

grapefruit
  cold comforter 154
  pink zinger 44
  watermelon sunset 106
grapes
  black grape fizz 120
  fruity refresher 38
  passionate magic 132
  sunshine smoothie 58
  white grape elderflower
    foam 146
  guava goodness 74

kiwi fruit
  cold comforter 154
  detox special 54
  fruity refresher 38
  kiwi cooler 144
  kiwi juice 148
  kiwi & lime shake 178

lemons
  homemade lemonade 122
  lemon surprise 110
  pink zinger 44
limes
  kiwi & lime shake 178
  pink zinger 44
mangoes
  detox special 54
  mango & orange smoothie 134
  melon & mango tango 98

smooth nectarine shake 182
tropical sunrise 16
maple syrup
  creamy maple shake 176
  fig & maple melter 206
melon
  fruity refresher 38
  green goddess 160
  honeydew 156
  melon & mango tango 98
  melon & pineapple crush 30
  melon refresher 138
  the reviver 82
  tropical watermelon
    smoothie 24
  wake-up juice 18
  watermelon sunset 106
  watermelon whizz 94

nectarines
  smooth nectarine shake 182
  sunshine smoothie 58

oranges
  apple cooler 108
  apricot buzz 104
  apricot & orange smoothie 66
  blood orange sparkler 162
  breakfast smoothie 8
  cold comforter 154
  maidenly mimosa 112
  mango & orange smoothie 134
  on the beat 88
  orange & strawberry cream 26
  peach & orange milkshake
    180
  sunrise crush 126
  tropical sunrise 16
  wake-up juice 18

papaya
  papaya & banana smoothie 52
  tropical smoothie 56
  tropical storm 186
passion fruit
  midsummer smoothie 198
  passionate juice fizz 116
  passionate magic 132
  pomegranate passion 114
peaches
  banana, peach & strawberry
    smoothie 36
  fruity refresher 38
  passionate magic 132
  peach bliss 190
  peach & orange milkshake 184
  pineapple tango 150
pears
  blueberry nectar 100
  elderflower & pear
    smoothie 152
  orchard fruit smoothie 40
  pear & raspberry delight 64
  red reviver 42
  spiced fruit boost 158
peppermint:
  iced coffee & chocolate
    crush 200
  peppermint refresher 196

peppers
  carrot & red pepper
    booster 48
  red pepper reactor 86
pineapple
  24 carrot 76
  coconut cream 194
  detox special 54
  fresh & fruity 102
  melon & pineapple crush 30
  perky pineapple 96
  pineapple tango 150
  strawberry & pineapple
    refresher 118
  sunrise crush 126
  tropical smoothie 56
  tropical storm 186
plums
  orchard fruit smoothie 40
  perfect plum shake 174
  plum fluff 188
  spiced fruit boost 158
pomegranates
  passionate juice fizz 116
  pomegranate passion 114
  tropical sunrise 16

raspberries
  berry booster 68
  blood orange sparkler 162
  breakfast berry smoothie 14
  forest fruit smoothie 130
  midsummer smoothie 198
  pear & raspberry delight 64
  raspberry & apple
    quencher 92
  raspberry & strawberry
    smoothie 28
  summer fruit slush 128
rhubarb: pink ginger shake 184

spinach
  green goddess 160
  rapid recharge 84
strawberries
  apple cooler 108
  banana & strawberry
    smoothie 50
  banana, peach & strawberry
    smoothie 36
  blood orange sparkler 162
  breakfast berry smoothie 14
  fruit kefir 34
  midsummer smoothie 198
  orange & strawberry cream
    26
  passionate magic 132
  peach bliss 190
  raspberry & strawberry
    smoothie 28
  strawberries & cream
    milkshake 168
  strawberry & pineapple
    refresher 118
  summer fruit slush 128

tomatoes
  red pepper reactor 86
  rise & shine juice 10